WITHOUT A HOMELAND
Irma Kurti

TRANSCENDENT ZERO PRESS
HOUSTON, TEXAS

Copyright © 2019, Irma Kurti.

PUBLISHED BY TRANSCENDENT ZERO PRESS
www.transcendentzeropress.org

All rights reserved. No part or parts of this book may be reproduced in any format whether electronic or in print except as brief portions used in reviews, without the expressed written consent of Transcendent Zero Press, or of the author Irma Kurti.

ISBN-13: 978-1-946460-13-4
Library of Congress Control Number: 2019938486

Printed in the United States of America

Transcendent Zero Press
16429 El Camino Real Apt. #7
Houston, TX 77062

Cover photo: Biagio Fortini
Graphic design: Glynn Monroe Irby

FIRST EDITION

WITHOUT A HOMELAND
Irma Kurti

Every love poem is dedicated to my parents:
Hasan Kurti and Sherife Mezini.

Using simple and linear language, the poet Irma Kurti offers us once again a babel of sensations through her stream of consciousness, a sort of diary in verse that opens the doors of reflection to intimate and existential themes. This collection consists of two parts that mark the transition from a more generic and kaleidoscopic vision of life to one of affection for loved ones.

Kurti cuts straight to the heart of the reader, embracing, as always, the idea that poetry is an instrument for the chosen few, because the narrative form, with its literary frills and artifice, does not align with her stylistic elements. Emotion itself speaks through memory, images, and thoughts, described in such a manner as to allow the reader to tiptoe into the author's life, without taking off their shoes.

Grazia Pia Licheri
Journalist

Table of Contents

Memories in Verse
I had forgotten the beauty / 11
A story will be extinguished / 12
The ticket / 14
Without a homeland / 15
The naked day / 16
A tired butterfly / 17
The wait / 18
Under the dark sky / 19
Beside a stream / 20
A kneeling world / 22
The morning knocks / 23
A melancholic music / 24
A star / 25
The long road / 26
The sun / 27
The same coin / 29
A danger / 30
Thirsty for time / 31
Being a woman / 32
Destiny / 33
The words on my lips / 34
A meteor / 35
Human theater / 36
I will not ask forgiveness / 37
Memories in verse / 39
Inside the old year / 40
The weather forecast / 42
A step away / 43
During the trip / 44
Tonight / 45
A soliloquy / 46
Old age / 47
A tumult of feelings / 48
What spring is this? / 50
The time unlived / 51

The hearts close / 52
I won't be silent / 53

This Love
Life drags on / 59
There are places / 60
I need you / 61
Ten years / 62
The weeping willow / 63
Two mothers / 64
The last dream / 65
A sky without stars / 69
Until dawn / 70
I miss your voice / 71
Drops of bliss / 72
This love / 73
My seasons / 74
I'm here / 75
A swallow without wings / 76
The last crumbs / 77
When I will lie in bed / 78
Not for a single instant / 79
Night without you / 80
The flame of a candle / 81
We met at dusk / 82
The lost soul / 84
Christmas verse / 85

MEMORIES IN VERSE

I had forgotten the beauty

I had forgotten your singular beauty,
the seas, the lakes, all the landscapes,
the parks, the nature, and the mountains
that from the hand of man remained safe.

Just today, in front of the television,
suddenly the embarrassment invaded me;
I didn't feel you part of me, it seemed
I was discovering you in that minute.

When I will set foot on your ground again
I won't carry any grudges from the past,
I'll free myself of those old regrets,
of the anguish that doubles the gap.

Slowly, I will place my head on a rock,
my body and my thoughts will get wet.
I will find a little bit of serenity in
fixing the flocks of birds in the sky.

And no one knows if I will ever pronounce
those words; I could never say,
on my skin a mixture of tears and waves:
"You know, I have really missed you!"

I had forgotten your singular beauty,
my country...

A story will be extinguished

One day we will close our eyes
in hospitals, foreign clinics,
far from family and the soil
that hold our best memories.
In that closure of the eyelids
a life will terminate forever,
just like within parentheses.

The grief will be annihilated,
the great nostalgia, the joys,
all the unfortunate endeavors
to preserve customs, traditions,
and save as a precious treasure
from the everyday life storms
our dear, suffering language.

The long, loud cries of sadness
that we have kept deep inside,
the rare delights under the sky,
whose blue didn't belong to us.
Prejudices of the petty beings
that we have swallowed like
morsels: bitter and difficult.

In our last isolated dwelling
there'll be a flower at least;
that pained and shapeless bud
will testify not only to our absence,
but to that of the family
and friends that couldn't come
and thus have forgotten us.

With the closure of eyelids
a story will be extinguished...

The ticket

I had planned to go
not just to meet people,
relatives and neighbors,
but to end my nostalgia
for my suffering earth.
Open doors and windows
of my childhood home
let the clean air enter
into each of its small rooms.

But now, I am stuck
in the trap of problems
that don't want to leave
me on this foreign soil,
so close and also beloved.
Who knows for how long
I'll exist like this,
with my soul hovering
in the air of two lands.

In my fingers lies inert
the ticket, this silent,
insignificant witness.
It slowly comes to life
from my distant memories;
it burns more than fire.
I stay with the wounded
spirit as the sky fills
its own chest with stars.

Without a homeland

What are you looking for on the shore,
shreds of memories or broken shells?
Seagulls to distant lands have flown,
abandoning thus their only love nest.

Just like you, who in a foreign land
tried to build with difficulty a roof.
Although from there, the cold, the rain,
nostalgia, and memories penetrate, too.

Nothing has remained, even that door
you opened in the dream of first love.
It was rusty, now it has been replaced
with a more beautiful and modern one.

You've changed also, you're a sky full
of clouds, hard to recognize yourself—
a sensitive soul, very often deluded;
a sad poetess, left without a homeland.

The naked day

It's early in the morning, my steps
are heard and all around are asleep.
The shop shutters will open slowly
like eyelids after a restless night.

I am calm and happy, the day's mine,
I might do with it anything I want;
fill it with many thoughts of light,
rotate it in my hands like a globe.

Then the streets begin to fill
with noises: the horns of the cars,
people hurry up, colliding with me.
The day escapes by my hands at once.

It undresses with the glee with which
I wrapped it. Now on the others it depends.
On its shoulders the stress crashes,
it slips from my fingers like a snake.

No more belongs to me the naked day.

A tired butterfly

I have often felt like a tired butterfly
that in the night crashes against a lamp,
beating its wings miserably on the glass,
though outside waits for it the universe.

I have fought lonely against my destiny,
and in a world of solutions, didn't find one.
Burned with disappointments without any
help, I wrapped around myself my arms.

And like a butterfly I fell to the ground,
I touched and embraced the frosty floor,
though flowers and horizons invited me,
although in the sky lots of stars shone.

The wait

You search in the multitude of emails
to find one that will change your life,
you cannot comprehend that this unkind
and hypocrite world donates you nothing.

The days are dragged like the turtles,
under the crooked lens of impatience,
you cannot distinguish even a sunray,
the horizons are obscured by the haze.

You've to fight every minute of life,
to get in return so little or naught,
so, let the days flow with serenity,
throw away the wait as a heavy stone.

Under the dark sky

I was looking up at the dark sky,
for so long I gazed at the stars,
as eyes in love they caressed me,
a lot of prayers burned inside of me.

Suddenly in my thoughts found space
for the many sufferings of this world,
of those who wake up with arms
or those who die under hunger's claw.

My body became soundless and light,
the sorrows diminished in a flash,
there're so many pains that mine
are insignificant in the universe.

And hence, my prayers expanded
under that dark and starry sky.

Beside a stream

I'm sitting beside
a torrent of water
that flows serenely,
it seems just like
a quick reptile
in the abundance
of the stones
and rocks.

My hands are
extended. I am
a beggar looking
for affection.
My thoughts
don't stay still,
they move and run
incessantly.

No one answers
my calls today.
The number flashes
on the screen
of the cell phone
like an insect
that is beating
its wings.

I do not know,
what to think
about my friends.
They are not
really far away,
and yet they're
lost without
leaving a trace.

Someone will come,
and drive away
my boredom like snow
from my sweater.
I'm sitting beside
the stream,
in silence I talk
with my thoughts.

A kneeling world

I had known this world from a distance:
sad eyes, melancholic, and really pensive,
people sitting on their wheelchairs and
lost in a thick fog of memories.

People who no longer recognize life,
its magic has turned into a nothingness,
their hair as white as snow on the roofs,
the pain like a knife that penetrates my soul.

The morning knocks

The morning knocks
even for those
that have desperation
in their eyes,
or a fridge
that looks like
an abyss to
those that
are fed each day
only on hope.

The morning knocks
also on the door
of the slow and
vulnerable people,
who fail to grab
their dreams
since they're faster
and suddenly
they escape
from their hands.

The morning knocks
even for those
prisoners
in their own beds,
who think and live
in the past;
they cannot order
their weary bodies
and they feel
like they're in a trap.

The morning knocks...

A melancholic music

My life
in these days
has the rhythm
of rock
music. I cannot
reflect or write
a single line,
in the mirror
I have no time
to watch
my portrait:
lost and tired.

A tune that
doesn't end
amidst the shouting
and the noise.
I cannot wait
until it slows down
and my life
takes on
another rhythm,
and sounds like
a light and
melancholic song.

A star

I would like
to scream at
this pain
that makes
me suffer.
The sun
no longer
warms me,
the moon
has impressed
its paleness
on my face.
The coldness
of the people
is a shiver
in my soul.

People
close
their ears,
and in the
madness
run to
seek meaning
in vain.
But above
my window
remains
motionless
a star.
I'll sew that
gold button
on my nightgown.

The long road

In front of me I've a very long road,
its end cannot be touched by my gaze;
in the twilight, I see a few people,
their bodies muted into shadows.

This will also be my path in the days
until I disappear into a colorless mark,
my track will be as slender as the thread
of a cloud left by a plane that flies.

But I wonder if the echo of my voice
will sound sweet and melodious too,
will it be like the scream of a raven
or the wind that softly caresses you?

In front of me I've a very long road,
its end cannot be touched by my gaze.

The sun

In a while
the sun
will rise
and the clouds
will dissipate
one by one,
so fast and
agitated
as if they felt
guilty for covering
the blue
by their gray.

In a while
the sun
will wake up
as a relaxed
eye. The strong
wind — a slap
on the cheeks
will become
a caress,
I will close
my eyelids
under the magic.

On the lips
will be drawn
a smile —
a musical
note. All
the pensive,
gloomy faces
will resemble
the opening
of timid buds,
in the first
days of spring.

Soon the sun
will rise.

The same coin

You have leaned on my shoulder
and cried for months and years,
you sprayed my days with poison,
I could never live my own bliss.

I understood too late: my life
no, didn't interest you at all,
my afflictions went in your ear
and out the other, of course.

You forgot the time I dedicated,
around you this world revolved.
If all I did wasn't worth it,
I'll use with you the same coin.

A danger

We are threatened by a great danger,
it's not an atomic bomb that destroys
all; it erodes the serenity and peace and
fills it with sadness, removes the words.

Loneliness — the lack of affection —
has created a spider's web in the soul,
while selfishness, vanity, fears,
and prejudices suffocate this world.

It's time to take off all the masks,
those that carry them for a lifetime,
then, the youth who recently use them
learning to live with hypocrisy, thus.

We are threatened by a great danger...

Thirsty for time

I'm thirsty for time.
In the days I look
for it desperately,
it slips from my hands
and burns my fingers
like friable sand.

I am a traveler,
I walk in the desert,
the infinity extends
like a white sheet,
it waits for me to write
verses or letters.

Thirsty for time ...

Being a woman

I have forgotten how to be a woman:
wear an elegant dress with high heels,
try to provoke someone with my charm,
put on makeup and apply lipstick.

With blue jeans and my sports shoes,
with my short hair I look like a boy,
with the certain and heavy step I am
a soldier that happily returns home.

Only my soul has not changed at all,
deep, it is measured in fathoms,
confused, capricious, and sensitive,
the vibrating string of instrument.

Destiny

Destiny, with the raven's profile,
stopped at the threshold of my house,
although I had closed the doors well
it found a way; it entered at once.

It measures sorrows and resistance,
bringing me problems that never end;
it checks if the rivers of my tears
will dry or if I will drown there.

Days pass and it doesn't abandon me,
from dreams and calm takes me away,
tries to mute the summer into winter
and the limpid dew in tears of pain.

Destiny, with the raven's profile,
stopped at the threshold of my house.

The words on my lips

All languages
of the world
are spoken
here. Only
my language
is not heard,
although
I open
my ears
just like
windmills.
Its letters
can't caress
my being.

For a few weeks,
I don't speak
it, there is
something
that I miss.
I start then
to sing,
and people think
I'm crazy.
The taste
of the honey
the words
leave on
my lips.

A meteor

There are people you would like to encounter
on your life's path at least once again,
touch their universe with slow fingers
and share an opinion, a smile together.

You have known them only for an instant
but they remain impressed on your mind,
permeate all your thoughts like lightning
and illuminate them like a meteor does the sky.

Human theater

This human theater of fake sentiments,
with lifeless looks and broken smiles,
who knows for how long it will go on,
I know it's killing me from time to time.

I am sure, somewhere there exist pure
feelings like the water of the stream;
they relax, enchant me, a real music,
to my heart eternal silence they give.

I will not ask forgiveness

I will not ask
forgiveness
from my country
for the anger
that invades me
when I step on
its land, for
the quarrels
with unknown
people,
for the few,
rare visits,
the nostalgia
and the absence
I don't feel.

I can't forget
those unlived
years
and the pains
of youth's first
blush ,
they chased me
quickly
to the sea,
pushing me.
They awaken me,
the wounds
every time,
I touch
its ground.

I will not ask
forgiveness
from my country.

Memories in verse

I'm trying
to transform
the memories
into verse
not to allow
them to wander
and get lost
in my mind
full of
problems.
Not to see
them burst
in the air
like some
soap bubbles.
I've lost
so many,
when I strive
to touch them,
they leave
dampness
in my hands.

Inside the old year

They have started now to decorate
all the trees along the boulevard,
the lights of the shop windows look
like blinking eyes.

And everything echoes in the songs,
through the noise and lots of publicity,
the old year, it is just one step
away from the time abyss.

I do not deny it, this year
for me has been long and difficult,
I wrapped myself in the affliction
as if inside a tight fist.

I would have enjoyed it like others,
would have danced with the stars,
would have shouted like that crowd
of children, teenagers, and adults.

I would have marked impatiently
on the calendar the remaining days,
I would have thrown my powerful
weapons: the pencil and paper.

How can I know whether the New Year
that everyone is waiting for,
will bring me many challenges,
or will be kind and obedient?

If the happiness will be little,
as if it came out of a dropper,
if it'll torment me, make me cry
from the lack of pleasures and joys.

I'm huddled up, protecting myself
within the old year, in silence.
I've become one with the sorrows
it has given me and the anxieties.

The weather forecast

The weather forecast
predicts an azure sky;
a very warm breeze
will blow. The sun
will rise early and
it will set late.

To enjoy the lovely
season, a blue sky
is not enough. You
must hold in your
soul the season
of spring and sun.

A step away

I don't know how I got here
with people who drink and speak too loud.
I'm a step away from the past errors
when like a fable I lived life.

The wine vibrates, wants to seduce me,
I am covering the glass with my hand,
my mind returns to the distant memories,
of alcohol and ease the smell.

My legs and my thoughts are shaking,
I'm on the threshold of drunkenness,
I'm not afraid of tonight, I'm scared
I will fall into sin as I did then.

During the trip

The soul fills
up slowly
during my trip,
with impressions
and desires,
with magical
and rare emotions,
with a thousand
perfumes, colors,
and it blossoms
like a tulip.

It was lukewarm
and had slowed
from the usual
frenetic pace.
It looked like
a dry well, dark
not very deep,
fed by
almost nothing
but the passage
of time.

The soul fills
up slowly
during my trip.

Tonight

No one answers me tonight
nobody answers my calls,
maybe, they are too busy
or they close their ears,
my name doesn't tell them
anything at all.

I wanted to exchange only
two words, because too many
make me tired. I wanted
to break all this silence
that has invaded me. Now
friendship has lost its charm.

A soliloquy

You're surrounded by a thousand smiles,
bright lights, lots of sweet words too,
meetings, greetings, praise, applause,
the world revolves around you.

And all this attracts and seduces you,
like the playground — a little child,
you don't understand that those people
only in front of your chair bow.

One day they will remove your armchair
without giving you time to understand,
you'll remain isolated as in a desert,
objects and people will evaporate.

The fake friends will turn their backs
on you. "Oh, how unfair this world is!"
Disillusioned, you'll enunciate loudly.
But the phrase will be a soliloquy.

Old age

Where did it end,
my strong and
unrestrained
desire
to have fun,
the deep shivers
of my spirit,
the sleepless
and turbulent
nights
for a love
that wasn't seen
on the horizon?

Where did it end,
my tendency
to find
new lands
between charm
and adventure?
Now I can
barely move;
I am in love
with the peace
and serenity.
Tell me, is this
old age?

A tumult of feelings

The journey
of return
in a train
that ran
on the tracks
of memories.
This foreign
country
waited for me
with rain,
in every drop
I felt
nostalgia on me.

On the doorstep
I looked for
the perfumes
and aromas
of furniture
and walls that
I had missed.
My absence
was sitting
on the grains
of dust
of emaciated
objects.

The heart—
a tumult
of feelings
is always,
many times
I belong
to two lands,
but often
I am helpless,
fragile;
I feel like
a naked body
on a winter's day.

What spring is this?

What spring is this
if the sun does not
warm you up,
like a piece of ice;
apathetic, distant,
and intact remains
the anima?

They publish photos
of mimosas,
the verses resemble
the rivers that flow;
this is a fake season—
spring does not need
publicity and noise.

The time unlived

Who will
 give back
 to me
 the time lost
 in vain,
 that lethargic
 sleep
 in which
 my country
 made me fall?

I would like
to have a day when
I'm not looking
for more.
I'll know how
to live it.
But the past
is blurred,
it fades away
like the fog.

Who will
 give back
 to me
 the time unlived ?

The hearts close

The walls rise up,
the borders are sealed,
hearts close like
hedgehogs. The afflicted
people have become one
with the sea and stones.

Beyond those walls
live so many,
selfish and cold, shy
and scared. The bliss
escapes from them while
they look for it in vain.

The walls rise up,
the borders are sealed,
hearts close like hedgehogs.
The world turns around
insensitive
to others' anguish.

The hearts close...

I won't be silent

I won't be
silent
until
there are
petty people
that upset
my sleep,
until
I'm surrounded
by people,
inert
and passive—
mannequins
locked up
at home
as they are behind
shop windows.

I won't be
silent
when I hear
pains that
scream, break
my chest,
when I see
the blood
that flows
in front of
others'
suffering.
If one day
it happens,
it means
that it is
my end.

THIS LOVE

Life drags on

Life drags on, life goes on
even after a painful and great loss,
the smile on the face is melancholic,
the colors are not the same anymore.

An emptiness like the hollow of an oak
in the heart, in the soul
it torments, ages you prematurely,
very often doesn't let you breathe.

Life continues although you'd want
to cry in the midst of the delight,
your most loved people aren't there
and nothing can be as it was.

Life drags on; life goes on.

There are places

There're places I won't visit again:
a city, a swimming pool, maybe a hotel,
a long road, the beaches of a lake or sea;
because they wake up pains in my chest.

We visited them a long time ago, when,
like the flowers of a bouquet,
we were inseparable, even in a dream,
lavishing each other with affection.

I cling to the memories with my nails
and in the days when the soul drips blood
we remain very few: one by one,
another star falls from my sky.

There're places I won't visit again,
although they offer a rare beauty.

I need you

Parents, now I need you so much more
than when I was little, just a child,
I fell, cried, took my first steps,
but with a lullaby I slept quietly.

In the hazy days or sleepless nights,
scared and vulnerable I really feel,
the world is a stranger, like a circus
of monkeys and wild beasts.

Ten years

Ten years without you,
without your caresses
and immense affection.
What vigorous waves
split us apart ?
The pain like a knife
hurt my soul, drowned
it in the emptiness.

Ten years. I do not
share my secrets
with anyone and thus
I've remained forever
hostage to the silence.
Happiness has lost
its magic, I cannot
hold it in my hands.

Ten years. I can't
hear your voice and
can't feel your love.
I exist in a body
without dreams, turn
into a shadow like you —
to meet again in one
eternal embrace, Mom.

The weeping willow

How long, Mom, since I have come to you?
The flowers have withered for sure,
the wild ones have grown very tall,
trying to infiltrate the immense blue.

I bow now before your memory,
like a child who has broken a glass,
and hides the misadventure by any means
in the limpid light of the sun.

My life has hit a crazy rhythm,
each day my steps hurry to run.
I have met so many of those masks
that threaten my thoughts and calm.

I lost the addresses of good people
and I can't find the sensitive ones.
I have lived days of rain and cold,
drops of tears remained in my eyes.

I don't want you to be part of this;
you spent many sleepless nights
with me. I'll close my eyelids and
in my memories I'll look for your hug.

Dear Mom, on your grave I will change
the flowers destroyed by the winter.
I'd like to offer it shadow in the summer,
I'd like to be your weeping willow.

Two mothers

Today the pain of a mother shocked me,
I felt her breathlessness and anxiety,
the desperation of losing her daughter,
all my tears joined hers so quietly.

I know that grief and affliction well
because it brings my mother to mind;
she didn't feel the pains in her body,
but for leaving me alone she suffered.

These mothers didn't know each other;
oh, they were thousands of miles away,
though to different languages they belonged
they would have become friends.

The love felt for children doesn't need
to be translated — it would unite them.
I cry mixed tears for that anonymous
mother and mine who like a vision vanished.

The last dream

Dear Mother.
You do not know
that you almost
came across
my love
on that gloomy
autumn day.
You were
departing
for your trip
without return,
and he, with his
hurried steps,
was coming
toward me.

If you had met,
you'd have been
really happy.
You would have
taken his hand
and with a soft
and firm voice
you'd have
told me:
"Listen honey,
 translate for me now,
 I would like
 to tell him
 two words that
 flow from the heart."

You would have
looked at him
for a long time
and
told him:
"I'm happy
to meet you,
I dreamed about
you a lot, like
every mother.
Try to love
my daughter.
She's so sweet
although she
can't show it.

She has a great
and turbulent
anima — it resembles
an ocean.
She believes
in people
so willingly and
then is
disappointed.
Very often she
doesn't sleep,
but that isn't
something new —
you already
knew.

I'll tell you
something: she
finds shelter
in her tears
even for one
single word.
When you see her
nervous, pensive—
don't bother her.
Leave her alone;
it will pass
soon.
She'll calm down
like a dark sea
after a storm.

Then she will
come to you
more tranquil
than ever and
you'll recognize
the love
that binds you.
Try to love her,
my son.
You are lucky
to have found her.
I don't tell you
this simply
because she's
my daughter."

Unfortunately,
for both of you
you couldn't meet.
Your path was
blurred by my
tears, for your
eternal journey.
After this
meeting
you would
have told me:
"I'm not afraid
to die anymore.
I have realized
my last dream."

A sky without stars

I promised that we would love one
another, when you left us forever.
The brittle twigs in a landscape
of winter, the promises resemble.

On the day when we exchange words,
the rancor breaks our peace again.
There's no harmony between us, though
the same blood flows in our veins.

Mom, the sun that warmed our souls
rose from your mere being once.
You always kept us close together—
your affection dominated our lives.

Now, in the world of your children
reigns a sky with no sun or stars.

Until dawn

Yesterday, I eavesdropped on your night
from a distance—it broke into parts.
I moved your illness into my own body;
I lived with your pain and discomfort.

I transferred your cough to my lungs;
my breath became heavy and difficult
for the effort and at the thought of you
my eyes immediately filled with tears.

Dad, I'd like to be with you until dawn;
share the anguish, slowly caress you,
travel to or touch with fingers the past—
the difficult years of your childhood.

I wanted to be with you until dawn...

I miss your voice

I miss your voice so much, Dad.
When our talks went on for hours;
that sweet music is only
an echo now.

I try to bring it back to memory,
it gets lost; it vanishes in the dark.
My gaze is wet with tears, I stay
close to you and I suddenly blush.

My first verses lay insecure, just
like dozens of buds in your hands
you seized them and chased away my fears,
for you were my best critic, Dad.

I didn't know there were diseases
that forever can steal the voice,
taking every word away from you,
the bridge that connected us both.

I'll translate your look into words,
I'll be pleased with the silence,
in my soul I'll keep as a rainbow
your sweet and unique smile.

I miss your voice so much, Dad...

Drops of bliss

In the morning I come to you
with some flowers in my hand,
time stops and all the noises
disappear at the same instant.

I trample a vast green field,
it reminds me of my childhood
when I created a big bouquet
and happily I gave it to you.

Dad, they were impoverished days,
hard to find even the flowers.
My heart — the helpless bird —
was nourished only with love.

Memories, perfumes are mixed;
unhappy thoughts leave me,
while the hospital's white room
is filled with drops of bliss.

This love

Loves that fade just when they are
born; others that don't find peace,
this one has a place in my spirit,
it's immense and infinite.

I'll fight against the cruel world,
on my shoulders I'll keep the rains,
I'll struggle against the intrigues,
in the river I'll throw them.

I'll protect you from the bad looks
and from the people's false kindness,
now that you are fragile, helpless,
and resemble an innocent child.

Loves that fade just when they are
born; others that don't find peace,
this one has a place in my spirit,
it's immense and infinite.

Dad...

My seasons

You see that lovely house on the hill
that has appeared like a giant mushroom?
I would like us to take refuge there,
far from this mad, chaotic world.

You'll cover my body with flowers,
you'll desire me in every white petal,
you'll caress me just like the breeze,
keeping my fragilities in your hand.

When the wind scatters the petals,
you'll recognize my autumn at once,
my youth lost in lines and wrinkles,
the sunset of faded charms.

You see that house? It seems unreal —
the backdrop of an ancient tale.
I'd like to live there through the seasons
for a year, a month, or a single day.

I'm here

Now I'm here,
close to you,
I'll not watch
the clock,
I won't follow
the crazy rush
of the hands
of time.

I'll caress
you as I never
did before,
my kisses
like lilies
will be
imprinted
on your skin.

A swallow without wings

Talking with you
on the phone
is difficult —
the sound
of the call
falls into a deaf
ear, my joy
undresses slowly
from the zeal.

The minutes pass,
even the hours —
the joy writhes,
shakes in the air,
it loses height,
like a swallow
without wings
it falls
to the ground.

The last crumbs

You greeted me with a kiss this morning
without suspecting for a single second
that now I don't sleep with your image.
There's no space for you in my reflections.

You won't look at me through the window,
while I am leaving with certain steps,
escaping from your thoughts and dreams
fading like a sun-bleached stain.

The way back is filled with fog and we
will not find each other there anymore.
The pigeons scattered everywhere peck at
the last crumbs of my sentiment.

When I will lie in bed

When I will lie in bed tired, exhausted,
the days and nights will seem to me equal,
the sorrow in my chest will make its nest.
I will throw away the multitude of drugs,
I will no longer fear their side effects.
I will use the only cure that is the best for me
but that no doctor would prescribe:
from the illness your kisses will save me.

When I will lie in bed tired, exhausted...

Not for a single instant

I won't be absent from your life
not even for a single instant.
I'll caress you, I'll decipher
your silences, your anxieties,
give you thousands of kisses.

I will never tire of you
and you will never hear my sigh.
If one day I am transformed
into your servant, it'll mean
that was my destiny.

Night without you

It's long
the night
without you,
divided into
splinters of time.
It dwells
on solitude,
on my dull
thoughts,
on the dreams
that look
for you
and we don't
share together.

The big bed
is all mine,
but it doesn't
belong to me,
it's so cold
and empty!
The hands
of the clock
slowly crawl
and bite into
my calm and
serenity —
the dawn is
far away.

The flame of a candle

This morning when I closed the door
and was hurrying off, almost numbed,
your portrait and the story we had
commenced to chase me like a ghost.

Our tempestuous past was a lizard,
from down the stairs, behind the parapet
it poked its head out and taunted me,
on your betrayals I slowly stepped.

I tried to change the course so that
positive thinking enlightened me,
your memory — the flame of a candle
flickered, languished as minutes passed.

I was reflecting on my fragilities,
the path was obstructed by the pain,
until that memory of you vanished
and the mist gradually cleared away.

We met at dusk

The two
of us met
at the dusk
of our lives,
we had wrinkles
on our faces
and gray hair
here and there.
We brought
with us
baggage
full of pains
and worries,
tears and
much more,
for which our house
did not have
enough space.

It happens
very often
that we wake up
at midnight,
without closing
our eyes again,
each of us perched
on the edge
of the bed,
moving closer
toward
one another.
What leaves
us sleepless—

the future
or the past?
No, neither
can answer aloud.

The lost soul

Days full
of clouds.
None of them
transmit
anything except
the silence
that breaks
between the sound
of the rain
falling on the ground.
My soul is lost;
it is listless
in the gray air.

Gloomy days
lacking
the shade
of sunrise.
Behind the glass
is expanded
a mute landscape.
And I count
the minutes
waiting for you.
You will draw
into your palms
my wandering soul.

Christmas verse

Beyond the window
covered with
fake snowflakes,
I hear the
monotonous beat
of heels
racing as fast
as horses,
the shrill sounds
of an orchestra,
the strange rush
to purchase
last-minute presents.

At the fireplace
we talk
with the stem of a glass
of red wine
between our fingers.
You read to me
poetry, on your
lips break up
the verses;
rhymes find
the quickest pathway
to penetrate
my anima.

Irma Kurti is an Albanian poetess, writer and journalist naturalized Italian. She is also well known as the lyrics writer of many famous Albanian songs. Her books have been translated into Italian and English. She has received numerous literary awards in Italy and Switzerland. In 2013, she won the IX Edition International Prize *Universum Donna* (equivalent to Woman of the Year) and the Ambassador of Peace nomination from the University of Peace in Lugano, Switzerland.

Irma Kurti has published seventeen books in Albanian language, eleven books in Italian and three in English. She lives in Italy.

www.ingramcontent.com/pod-product-compliance
Lightning Source LLC
Chambersburg PA
CBHW032209040426
42449CB00005B/502